WHY AM I HERE?
HOW DID I GET HERE?
WHERE AM I GOING?

THE CONCEPT OF DESTINY

JOHN OWOADE AGBOOLA

Trilogy Christian Publishers

A Wholly Owned Subsidiary of Trinity Broadcasting Network

2442 Michelle Drive

Tustin, CA 92780

Copyright © 2024 by John Owoade Agboola

Scripture quotations marked KJV are taken from the King James Version of the Bible. Public domain. Scripture quotations marked BBE are taken from the Bible in Basic English. Public domain. Scripture quotations marked ESV are taken from the ESV® Bible (The Holy Bible, English Standard Version®), copyright © 2001 by Crossway Bibles, a publishing ministry of Good News Publishers. Used by permission. All rights reserved. Scripture quotations marked NKJV are taken from the New King James Version®. Copyright © 1982 by Thomas Nelson. Used by permission. All rights reserved. Scripture quotations marked ISV are taken from the International Standard Version. Copyright ©1995-2014 by ISV Foundation. All rights reserved internationally. Used by permission of Davidson Press, LLC. Scripture quotations marked ERV are taken from the Easy-to-Read Version, copyright © 2006 by Bible League International.

All rights reserved, including the right to reproduce this book or portions thereof in any form whatsoever.

For information, address Trilogy Christian Publishing

Rights Department, 2442 Michelle Drive, Tustin, CA 92780.

Trilogy Christian Publishing/ TBN and colophon are trademarks of Trinity Broadcasting Network.

For information about special discounts for bulk purchases, please contact Trilogy Christian Publishing.

Trilogy Disclaimer: The views and content expressed in this book are those of the author and may not necessarily reflect the views and doctrine of Trilogy Christian Publishing or the Trinity Broadcasting Network.

10 9 8 7 6 5 4 3 2 1

Library of Congress Cataloging-in-Publication Data is available.

ISBN 979-8-89041-893-7

ISBN 979-8-89041-894-4 (ebook)

"Before I made you in your mother's womb, I knew you. Before you were born, I chose you for a special work" (Jeremiah 1:5 ERV).

"My frame was not unseen by you when I was made secretly, and strangely formed in the lowest parts of the earth. Your eyes saw my unformed substance; in your book all my days were recorded, even those which were purposed before they had come into being" (Psalm 139:15-16 BBE).

DEDICATION

This book is dedicated to you who are reading this book. To your success in life, to your guaranteed satisfaction with living, and to a great sense of fulfillment at the end of your days. It is also dedicated to my number-one mentor and cheerleader: my mom, Felicia Olajoke Agboola. "May you spend the rest of your days in prosperity, and the years in pleasures."

CONTENTS

INTRODUCTION 1

PART 1 5
WHY ARE YOU HERE?

CHAPTER 1 7
IT IS NEVER TOO LATE TO DISCOVER PURPOSE

CHAPTER 2 13
FULFILLMENT IN LIFE BEGINS WITH
THE DISCOVERY OF PURPOSE

CHAPTER 3 17
IS THERE A FIXED DESTINY?

CHAPTER 4 23
WHATEVER WILL BE WILL BE

CHAPTER 5 27
YOUR DESTINY IS IN YOUR HANDS (NOT EXACTLY!)

CHAPTER 6 31
I DETERMINE MY OWN DESTINY (CAUTION, MY DEAR!)

CHAPTER 7 37
HOW TO FULFILL YOUR DESTINY - A

CHAPTER 8 41
HOW TO FULFILL YOUR DESTINY - B

CHAPTER 9 45
HOW TO FULFILL YOUR DESTINY - C

CHAPTER 10 51
HOW TO FULFILL YOUR DESTINY - D

CHAPTER 11 55
HOW TO FULFILL YOUR DESTINY - E

CHAPTER 12 59
    WHAT IS WRITTEN CONCERNING YOU?

CHAPTER 13 63
    THE MOST IMPORTANT VARIABLE
    IN THE EQUATION OF YOUR LIFE

CHAPTER 14 67
    WHICH IS THE MOST IMPORTANT BOOK
    TO BE WRITTEN ABOUT YOU?

YOU WERE BORN A KING; DO NOT DIE A PEASANT! 71

CONTACT THE AUTHOR: 75

INTRODUCTION

It was still a long while before dawn when Abraham woke Isaac up from sleep and nudged him to get dressed. The little boy was oblivious of what lay ahead on that fateful day, but on the final lap of that journey, the servants were left at the foot of Mount Moriah while the wood was handed over to Isaac and his father. Abraham handled the torch. At that moment, a question came to the young mind: "Dad, something is missing here. Behold, the fire and the wood, but where is the lamb for the sacrifice?" But his dad could not come up with a satisfactory answer. By the end of the day, Isaac had understood that the purpose for his life was to be a living sacrifice unto God. To be successful, he was to live a life given unto God.

The Concept of Destiny

God, who made the whole universe and placed human beings on one of the planets, has a big picture in His mind, and the best an individual can do is to fit into it. However, people have been on the venture of overseeing their own destiny without God. In this venture, we have achieved a lot, yet we do not seem to be doing a good job. There is more confusion, and a lot of trouble all over the globe, than ever before.

One pertinent question in the heart of all human beings is the question, "What is the purpose for my existence?" That is the question for everything that was made. If there were a new invention today, the first question the inventor would need to answer is the question of purpose. The primary purpose of a car is mobility, and to achieve this it has an engine and its components, which are coupled to the wheels. However, the car would not be complete without the cabin and comfortable seats on the inside. Every individual component of the car has a unique purpose in the overall purpose of mobility. A moving car without comfort, safety, and security of the occupants is not complete. In the same way, we all exist as components of a bigger picture, and none is more important than the other in accomplishing our individual tasks. Each of us must succeed in our role for the world to be a better place.

"Before I made you in your mother's womb, I knew you. Before you were born, I chose you for a special work..." [1]

Jeremiah was still very young when God revealed to him his purpose. David was a lad when he realized that he was going to be a king someday. Joseph was still a kid when he discovered that he would become a mighty ruler. It may not be written in the sky or on a slate, and there may not be a prophet or a dream, but one thing is clear: you were made for a purpose, and your life is fulfilled when you accomplish it. This is true even when you do not know God. The birth and purpose of Cyrus, the great Persian

---

1   Jeremiah 1:5 (ERV)

Introduction

king, was declared hundreds of years before he was born. Yet he did not know God.

"Thus says the LORD to his anointed, to Cyrus, whose right hand I have grasped, to subdue nations before him... 'I will go before you and level the exalted places... I will give you the treasures of darkness and the hoards in secret places, that you may know that it is I, the LORD, the God of Israel, who call you by your name.

"For the sake of my servant Jacob, and Israel my chosen, I call you by your name, I name you, though you do not know me. I am the LORD, and there is no other, besides me, there is no God; I equip you, though you do not know me, that people may know, from the rising of the sun and from the west, that there is none besides me; I am the LORD, and there is no other.'" [2]

It suffices to say that there is a purpose for our existence as a people, and there is a definite or specific purpose for each person. Many have chosen for themselves a reason for living; some have been given a purpose by others; while a few have discovered the specific reason in the heart of the Creator for their individual existence. Have you found your purpose? When you do, you will experience a sense of purpose, and in the pursuit thereof, a lot of adventure and lasting peace.

In this book you will discover a fresh understanding of destiny as exemplified in the scriptures. The emphasis will be on fulfilling the purpose of your existence as an individual. While God has a purpose for all of mankind, in that big picture is a purpose for every individual. More often, this is referred to appropriately as *destiny*. In this book you will discover that destiny is not a point of arrival; rather, destiny is a journey of purpose, and on that journey there are several destinations.

In the Bible, we realize that the purpose of the creation of man was relationship. God wanted men on the earth who would be in constant communion with him. With direct access to the

---
[2] Isaiah 45:1-6 (ESV)

The Concept of Destiny

mind of God, man would reign on the earth by exhibiting the influence of heaven on the earth. Man was to have dominion on the earth while maintaining a union with God. Man lost this union, but God worked out a way to restore the relationship through Christ Jesus. Jesus Christ the Savior came to the earth with the sole purpose of seeking out those who are able to worship God in spirit and in truth.

"But the time is coming when the true worshipers will worship the Father in spirit and truth. In fact, that time is now here. And these are the kind of people the Father wants to be his worshipers. God is spirit. So the people who worship him must worship in spirit and truth." [3]

To fulfill this goal, God the Father took the first step of reaching out to man. When we accept the finished work of Christ, our spirit, the inward man, comes alive. We are transformed by the Spirit of God (getting into the same realm with God) and are able to relate with God in such a way that pleases Him, and by that we become empowered to exercise our dominion on the earth.

How does a man discover purpose? How does a man fulfill the purpose for his life? What exactly is destiny? I do not claim to have all the answers, but we could take a walk together through the Bible (the library of books). Do come along on this interesting journey of discovery.

*Read Genesis 22:2-19

---

3   John 4:23-24 (ERV)

PART 1
WHY ARE YOU HERE?

CHAPTER 1
IT IS NEVER TOO LATE TO DISCOVER PURPOSE

Are you on the path of purpose?

God promised Abraham a seed, and through that seed, his generation would become a mighty nation through which all the nations on the earth would be blessed. That seed was the seed of promise which came through Sarah, his legally married wife. Thus, it suffices to say that God knew that Isaac would be born before he was born, and the purpose was to carry on a legacy of fulfilling the Abrahamic covenant. That could be termed

The Concept of Destiny

"predestination," meaning that Isaac had a purpose for his life which he was to fulfill right from birth. This *purpose* is often referred as "destiny." *

King Saul was in the second year of his reign when God rejected him. God later told Samuel the prophet that He had found for Himself another man who was preferred to Saul and who would replace him as the King of Israel. Years later, Samuel was instructed to anoint David as king over Israel.

Apparently, David was not yet born when God rejected Saul. However, David was just thirty years old by the time Saul died, thirty-eight years after the prophecy. This reveals that at the time God spoke concerning David, he was still a seed in the loins of his father Jesse. David was predestined to be a king, eight years before his birth! **

There is a purpose for everything in creation. Science has unearthed the purpose for many things in life, and yet not all purpose has been discovered or fully defined. In ecology, we create the pyramid that reveals at what level each animal belongs and how they work together to sustain the circle of life. In our body, we have depicted the purposes of the different parts of the brain. And we have tried to explain the role of the different systems that make up our body. Every designer, inventor, artist, or manufacturer defines the purpose of their project, invention, music, artwork, or product and makes an effort to ensure customer satisfaction. The same way that the success of a product leads to the glory of the manufacturer, your success in life leads to God's glory and praise. You were formed with a purpose in mind, and your life has a destiny to accomplish. Have you discovered this overarching goal of your existence?

I am engaging in this discussion on the topic of destiny premised on the scriptures, which for this purpose will be the Holy Bible. The Holy Bible makes it clear that there is an omnipotent force, the Creator, and He is the Almighty God who made the heavens and the earth. This book on destiny is based on the fact that there is a creative and intelligent mind who made the heavens and the earth and all that is therein. That creative mind, which is God, has an intent and purpose for everything and anyone that He brings to existence. His purpose for each person can be regarded as their destiny or purpose.

"For you formed my inward parts; you knitted me together in my mother's womb. I praise you, for I am fearfully and wonderfully made. Wonderful are your works; my soul knows it very well. My frame was not hidden from you, when I was being made in secret, intricately woven in the depths of the earth. Your eyes saw my unformed substance; in your book were written, every one of them, the days that were formed for me, when as yet there was none of them." [1]

At a tender age, between the ages of five to nine years, these questions came to my young mind: Why am I here? What is my purpose? What am I meant to achieve? Except for youngsters whose future has been laid up for them from childhood—like those born into royalty, a specific lineage, an established family craft, or prodded into a specific sport/career from childhood—I have met many young people who begin to question their purpose of existence in their teenage years. My children also began to have similar questions within the same age bracket.

---

1   Psalm 139:13-16 (ESV)

The Concept of Destiny

"O LORD, I know that the way of man is not in himself: it is not in man that walketh to direct his steps." [2]

"How can a young person live a pure life? By obeying your word." [3]

The Word of God is the manual of life. Who else could write a manual for creation if not the Creator? The Word of God is the "super" book. If you would seek to find God's purpose for your life, if you would do this with all your heart, you will find it. He is thinking about you, and His thoughts concerning you are precious thoughts. I advise that you cease from your own wisdom and turn to Him today.

"'I say this because I know the plans that I have for you.' This

---

2   Jeremiah 10:23 (KJV)
3   Psalm 119:9 (ERV)

It is Never Too Late To Discover Purpose

message is from the LORD. 'I have good plans for you. I don't plan to hurt you. I plan to give you hope and a good future. Then you will call my name. You will come to me and pray to me, and I will listen to you. You will search for me, and when you search for me with all your heart, you will find me.'" [4]

As a young man or woman, boy or girl, walking through this wild world, it takes light to navigate our way. My intention through this book is to share with you the discovery of purpose based on what is written in the Word of God. Ensure that you read to the end!

"Thy word is a lamp unto my feet, and a light unto my path." [5]

*Read Genesis chapters 15-18

**Read 1 Samuel chapters 13:1-14, 16, & 2 Samuel 5:4

---

4   Jeremiah 29:11-13 (ERV)
5   Psalm 119:105 (KJV)

CHAPTER 2
FULFILLMENT IN LIFE BEGINS WITH THE DISCOVERY OF PURPOSE

There is a purpose for your life.

One could say that Joseph came late to the scene because his mother was barren, and she sought desperately for a child without success for a very long time. Rachel never gave up, and the time came when she got pregnant and gave birth to Joseph, Jacob's eleventh son. The coming of Joseph changed everything in the whole family.

As a young child, Joseph began to have dreams which foretold his future. While the dreams were not so clear to Joseph himself, his father, who had a lot of experience with dreams, was his tutor in the interpretation of those dreams. The summary of the dreams

The Concept of Destiny

was that Joseph would be a ruler one day. He was going to be in such a great position that even his father and brothers would be compelled to bow before him. This destiny had been declared over a hundred years before his birth, and Joseph fulfilled his destiny. *

"Before I made you in your mother's womb, I knew you. Before you were born, I chose you for a special work. I chose you to be a prophet to the nations." [1]

Jeremiah was told by God that before he was formed in his mother's womb, he had been known to God and was ordained to be a prophet unto the nations. Jeremiah grew up amidst a lot of conflicts. In his day, almost no one was interested in God or what He had to say. Individuals made themselves gods and set up clichés and authoritarian groups that established wickedness in the community. Divine laws were set aside, and rulers made up laws which entrenched them perpetually in charge of the land and deprived the people of their possessions. Yet, God told Jeremiah, "Say whatever I tell you to say. No one will be able to harm you because I am God, and I am sending you." Jeremiah succeeded in his life mission. **

A builder would not start building a house until the design was ready. This design would have been in the imagination of the architect before being drawn, sketched, or modelled into what can be seen. In other words, the building was already completed in someone's imagination before the actual building began. The same goes for clothes made by a designer. It must have been seen in the imagination of the seamstress before being produced as a real copy. In the same vein, no car or machine is produced until the perfect design, purpose, and capacity have been concluded. If we as human beings do this routinely, it is because we were created in the image of the Creator.

It is clear from scriptures and from the nature of man that God does not do a thing unless He has completed it in His mind. Every child that is being formed in the womb, even before

---

[1] Jeremiah 1:5 (ERV)

There is a Purpose for Your Life

the mother realized she was pregnant, already has his destiny determined by the Creator. Each person has a role to play in life, in the community we find ourselves in, and in the world at large. Our roles vary; some are leaders in one sphere or another, others are to play supportive roles, some are to be followers or part of a team, while others are to nurture, coach, or train great leaders. No single role is greater than the other.

None should envy another, nor desire to play a role he/she was not defined for. Setting up an individual—one person—as a role model and following blindly has immensely fuelled the confusion we see around us. Many people are trying to be copies of others instead of being the original they were meant to be. We have an abundance of "counterfeit persons" who live the life they really do not want to live but have been made to believe that it is the ideal life.

Do I suppose that we automatically fulfill our destiny? Do I pretend to imagine that God's plans and purposes over individual lives and nations do not fail? No. Often, God's purposes for our lives fail; and when they succeed, it is not usually according to His perfect plan.

The point is that regardless of the circumstances surrounding your birth or the place of your birth, there is a divine agenda over your life. In other words, the Creator has a great plan for your life. The first assignment in life is to discover that purpose and to be set on the path of fulfilling it.

"It is the glory of God to conceal a thing: but the honour of kings is to search out a matter" [2]

You were born a king, meant to reign and dominate in your realm of life. It is your honor to discover purpose.

*Read Genesis chapters 35-41

**Read Jeremiah chapter 1

---

2   Proverbs 25:2 (KJV)

CHAPTER 3
IS THERE A FIXED DESTINY?

What direction are you facing?

"Samuel said, 'You did a foolish thing. You did not obey the LORD your God. If you had done what he commanded, the LORD would have let your family rule Israel forever. But now your kingdom won't continue. The LORD was looking for a man who wants to obey him. He has found that man—and the LORD has chosen him to be the new leader of his people, because you didn't obey his command.'" [1]

---

1 1 Samuel 13:13-14 (ERV)

The Concept of Destiny

Saul was the first King of Israel appointed by God. He was God's first choice, and his family would have reigned over Israel forever, but Saul missed it by a long stretch because of his attitude and decisions. David was God's alternate choice, and he succeeded in establishing his throne for generations to come. Saul's decisions affected Jonathan, his son, who was destined by birth to be king after his father.

The generation of Israel that left Egypt for Canaan never got there. They had been pre-determined by God to inherit the land promised to them through His covenant with Abraham, but they never possessed it. They failed to fulfill their destiny as planned and as revealed by God to Abraham, four hundred years before they were born. It was their children, born to them in the wilderness and who had never been circumcised, who inherited the promised land. It is evident that while God never changes His purposes, He may change His plans inclusive of who to use. [2]

There is the concept of *destiny* which says that we were pre-destined before we were born, and no matter what we do about it, we cannot change it. I bluntly disagree. I do that, however, with serious caution, because there are some very significant exceptions. We need to take note, however, that exceptions are not the rule.

Destiny talks about destination and can be predicted based on the direction you are facing. A man facing the east would not end up in the west; neither will a man facing the south end up in the north. A man learned in science may not become an artist except there is a course change. Likewise, even though it is expressed in scriptures that God has a predetermined purpose for each person, our choices in life could clearly dictate in which path our destiny lies.

For the purposes of this book, I would define *destiny* in two concepts as: the predetermined end point; or the end result of all decisions made (sum of effects) during the course of a

---
[2] Numbers chapter 14

Is There a Fixed Destiny?

lifetime. Therefore, no matter what God had in mind at your creation, you will decide if it comes to pass or modify how it would come to pass. God and you are not the only factors, but even your environment and other significant persons have a role in the fulfillment of your God-ordained destiny.

For example, for every cigarette a man smokes, he deducts seven minutes from his lifetime. Not only that, but he also increases the chances of dying of cancer or other severe, debilitating diseases. While this may not happen to all smokers, it is more likely than with non-smokers. Thus, choosing to smoke a cigarette or its adaptations pre-destines a person to the possibility of a shorter lifespan. Does that have to do solely with God? No. Therefore, when we consider events on the earth, it is not only God who brings things to be. There are co-creators!

If you are alive, you are moving with time in a particular direction; every decision you make leads to a particular end result. The direction you are facing—by this I mean your choices, lifestyles, decisions, habits, attitude, and relationships—ultimately determines where you will end and how you will end up.

Thus, there is the original plan or purpose of God the Creator, which has been predetermined before birth, and the modified plan, which is because of activities of other agents on the earth such as parents, governments, community, Satan and his agents, etc.

Our parents made decisions which affected us while we were young. They decided which schools we attended, where we lived, and the neighborhood in which we lived. The laws of our nation affected our circumstances, as our citizenship afforded us certain rights and expectations. Satan and his agents have often made efforts to destroy God's counsel and plans for our lives. For example, Herod tried to kill baby Jesus, Joseph's brothers would have killed him, and David had opportunity to kill Saul and was really tempted to do so, but he did not.

Ultimately, if we are lucky to live long enough to start making our own decisions as we become independent, then we

The Concept of Destiny

become responsible for our own actions. Thus, the final plan or the end (destiny) is not completed until all these factors have played their role.

Therefore, while there is a destiny as predetermined by God, the actual end (destiny) is determined by several factors, so that ultimately the individual plays a major role in determining his own fate.

Sometimes we try to make it look as if we had no choice in the matter, but the truth is that several persons have passed through worse conditions than you are passing through, and they found the inner strength to make certain different decisions from yours, and they ended well.

The road to the fulfillment of destiny is equally as important as the predetermined end. Samson failed, in the case of Delilah. God's original plan for his life did not materialize as planned. Though God dealt with the Philistines through Samson's hands as promised, he was not meant to die the way he did. [3]

Mephibosheth was Saul's grandson. After Saul, Jonathan would have been king, if his father had made the right decisions and obeyed God's instructions. Mephibosheth lost the opportunity to become king because his father would no longer be king. Yet his future was already secured through the covenant between David and Jonathan. However, he became lame as a little child, from complications which occurred when his aunt was fleeing with him. [4]

Finally, we may say that there is destiny, but this is not guaranteed until played out! Destiny can change, fail, or be modified. We always have an important role to play in it. A change of direction, a little modification of lifestyle, and a sudden change of mind can all alter the course of our lives and our destiny. Will you take responsibility for yours today?

---

[3] Judges chapter 16
[4] 2 Samuel 4:4, 9:6-11

Is There a Fixed Destiny?

"*Jabez was more honourable than his brothers; and his mother called his name Jabez, saying, 'Because I bore him in pain.' Jabez called upon the God of Israel, saying, 'Oh that you would bless me and enlarge my border, and that your hand might be with me, and that you would keep me from harm so that it might not bring me pain!' And God granted what he asked.*"[5]

---

5   1 Chronicles 4:9-10 (ESV)

CHAPTER 4
WHATEVER WILL BE WILL BE

There is a popular saying that "Whatever will be will be." It teaches the need not to worry about tomorrow and helps to deal with anxiety regarding the future. It is a good attitude not to worry about the future, because no one is sure of what tomorrow may bring. However, there is a need to do the right things today, and meeting the demands that life may place on us. We have roles to play and purposes to fulfill within our short time here on earth.

We all have a role to play in our daily lives. We have decisions to make concerning ourselves, our relationships, and our community.

The Concept of Destiny

The cumulative effects of our personal decisions, and those of others around us, all work together to determine our end.

Samson was born at a prime time when Israel needed a deliverer. His birth was foretold, and his parents prepared for his coming. Samson had a covenant with God, and he became so strong that he was a "one-man army." He was a terror to the enemies of Israel. Samson, however, had a problem: he always loved strange women. God had no problem with this, and in fact, it gave him opportunities to deal ruthlessly with the enemies of his nation. One day, Samson took an action which got him out of his divine covenant with God. At that moment, God's presence left, and Samson became an ordinary man.

"He told her all his heart, and said unto her, there hath not come a razor upon mine head; for I have been a Nazarite unto God from my mother's womb: if I be shaven, then my strength will go from me, and I shall become weak, and be like any other man." [1]

His parents had played their part well. God had played his part well in keeping the terms of the covenant, which included an immediate answer to every prayer; but ultimately, Samson determined his end. His decisions ordered the course of his life, which played out differently from what God had planned.

"For, lo, thou shalt conceive, and bear a son; and no razor shall come on his head: for the child shall be a Nazarite unto God from the womb: and he shall begin to deliver Israel out of the hand of the Philistines." [2]

Samson had broken several laws as an individual and had taken them for granted. He was not just a Jew, but a Nazarite. He was not supposed to touch any dead thing. However, he touched the carcass of a lion. He was not meant to marry a non-Jew, but he chose to, and even went to prostitutes. Do I have a problem with anything he did? No. He was free to make his choices, but

---

1   Judges 16:17 (KJV)
2   Judges 13:5 (KJV)

his decisions mattered a lot to his destiny. The question to ask is whether Samson understood that the woes which befell him were a result of his own actions. We are not told if he did. What we know is that he focused on what had befallen him, and considering the shame and reproach, he pleaded with God to end his life and God granted his request. *

"All the days of the vow of his separation there shall no razor come upon his head: until the days be fulfilled, in the which he separateth himself unto the LORD, he shall be holy, and shall let the locks of the hair of his head grow." [3]

In many instances, whatever befalls us in life has a lot to do with our own decisions, indecisions, actions, and inactions. While the decisions and the actions of others may affect us, may we realize that our lifestyle and actions matter the most. Our choices have different outcomes and can change the course of our lives. Therefore, "whatever will be" will not always be.

*Read Numbers chapter 6

---

[3] Numbers 6:5 (KJV)

CHAPTER 5
YOUR DESTINY IS IN YOUR HANDS (NOT EXACTLY!)

Many forces are at play in our lives. We are not always in charge. Sometimes we need a force outside of us to work in our favour. A lot of times there are external forces that exert very strong influences which either maximize our efforts or make them futile, no matter how much we try,

"Again I saw that under the sun the race is not to the swift, nor the battle to the strong, nor bread to the wise, nor riches to the intelligent, nor favor to those with knowledge, but time and chance happen to them all." [1]

---

1   Ecclesiastes 9:11 (ESV)

The Concept of Destiny

Is that a basis for resigning to fate? Not at all, because life—most of the time—gives room to those who insist on what they want and are clear about it. If one is in pursuit of a clear vision, more often than not, other forces either align or succumb to the person. At the end, only very few can blame external factors for the outcome of their lives.

"Whatever your hand finds to do, do it with all your might." [2]

Life is like a game of cards. We do not determine the series or how the cards come our way. Life deals the cards, while we decide how to play to win!

We can say of Reuben, Jacob's son, that he was unlucky. He was brought up in a compound with so many people, in a setting comprised of his grandpa, dad, mom, stepmoms, uncles, aunts, cousins, siblings, stepsiblings, servants, and many more. The house was full of so much strife, and his father was so busy working for grandpa that he was barely around. Reuben grew up among "the boys" with not much of a father's tutoring.

However, it was still an act of personal will for him to lure his father's concubine to bed. Yes, he must have been greatly influenced by the environment in which he grew up, but no one forced him to go up to his father's bed. We should note that he was not the only person who grew up in that environment, but among the other siblings, he was the only one recorded to have gone to his father's bed. [3]

We could say that Joseph was different compared to Reuben; he was born at a time when his father had gained independence. For Joseph, home was more of a nuclear setup, comprised mainly of his dad, mom, stepmoms, siblings, and servants. There were no uncles, aunts, cousins, grandpa, etc. Evidently, his father also had more time with him. Jacob could give him the attention of a father while his older sons took care of the animals.

---

2   Ecclesiastes 9:10 (ESV)
3   Ecclesiastes 9:10 (ESV)

Your Destiny is in Your Hands (Not Exactly!)

Joseph was a boy one could have described as a delicately brought up or "spoiled" child, until he was sold into slavery. However, Joseph consistently made right choices and exhibited chastity, even when he was far from home with no one watching him. He decided to stay faithful to the ideals he had learned at home without deviating from them, and he was honored at the end of it all. [4]

In life, the sociocultural attributes of the community in which we live, the laws guiding our nation, the attitude of others to our race or lineage, and the other ideals we imbibe all go a long way to influence us. We cannot afford to take this for granted. Nevertheless, we must take responsibility for our outcome. We must not leave our life to chance. We must do what it takes to end well.

Most importantly, we must learn how to court the right influences to work in our favor. There is a need to imbibe the right attitudes, which will endear us to helpers of destiny. We must learn how to form the right network, which will propel us in the direction we desire to go. Ultimately, consciously or subconsciously, most of the time you are the one to choose how you will end. The remaining few times are exceptions, and exceptions are not the rule!

"Blessed is the man who walks not in the counsel of the ungodly, nor stands in the path of sinners, nor sits in the seat of the scornful; but his delight is in the law of the LORD, and in His law he meditates day and night. He shall be like a tree planted by the rivers of water, that brings forth its fruit in its season, whose leaf also shall not wither; and whatever he does shall prosper." [5]

---

4   Genesis 30:22-43 and chapters 37, 39-40
5   Psalm 1:1-3 (NKJV)

CHAPTER 6
I DETERMINE MY OWN DESTINY (CAUTION, MY DEAR!)

Many become so successful in their endeavours that they become proud in their assertions, assume sole responsibility for their achievements, and claim the credit. When this happens to a person, it often leads to their destruction. There is nothing you have that you have not been given.

"*A man can receive nothing, except it be given him from heaven.*" [1]

Your life, your brain, your beauty, your lineage, and the money you earned or inherited are all gifts. Everything about you, including what you think you merited, is only yours because it was given to you. So, if it was given to you, why do you take credit for it?

---
1   John 3:27 (KJV)

The Concept of Destiny

If all things are working out for you as planned, based on your carefully thought-out schemes and due to your "smartness," if you can see the direct results of your hard work translated into magnified achievements beyond imagination, and if you can account it to nothing else but your efforts at being responsible, congratulations to you.

However, if that makes you think that you are ultimately in control of the consequences of your actions and you begin to take the law into your hands and to exalt yourself beyond your capacity, you must tread carefully, because destruction is just around the corner.

The Babylonian king, Nebuchadnezzar, ruled the world for a time. He achieved much more than any king before him. Nations crumbled before his armies, and several were taken captive and sent into exile. This he did to ensure that those nations no longer existed as a nation but were scattered all over his territory as peoples, but not as nations.

Thus, he decimated nations and exerted his rule over the whole world as it existed at that time. All the greatness of those kingdoms and the wisdom thereof combined made his kingdom strong, beautiful, and majestic to behold. After all these, pride entered his heart, and he attributed his success to himself and elevated himself to the position of a god. It was at that peak that his destruction came. His kingdom was taken from him, and he became a beast and was sent off into the forest to learn humility.[2]

"Pride goes before destruction, and a haughty spirit before a fall."[3]

---

2   Daniel chapter 4
3   Proverbs 16:18 (NKJV)

I Determine My Own Destiny (Caution, My Dear!)

It becomes a dangerous thing when men feel they can determine the consequences of their actions. The power given to man is to make the right decisions and to enjoy the consequences thereof. Consistent alignment with the laws of life and nature, making right decisions per time, and following through with those decisions more often than not will result in great successes. Repeated successes in one's endeavors makes one great.

However, success in a wicked endeavor does not guarantee that one can control the consequences of his actions. The day you make a wrong decision and you get away by manipulating your way out of the consequences thereof, life gets tilted out of balance. For every wrong and wicked act, there are consequences. If you manipulate your way successfully out of the consequences of a wicked act, somebody else is made to pay for it. If you pride yourself on the fact that you have become cunningly smart enough to wriggle your way out of the consequences of your wicked acts, destruction ultimately awaits you at the end, and that may involve your generations yet unborn.

The Concept of Destiny

Cain offered a wrong sacrifice and was rejected. He felt bad about it. The right reaction would have been to change his lifestyle and do the right thing. Instead of doing this, he killed his own brother who was doing what was right. Abel's life was cut short because of his brother trying to evade the consequences of his own wrong action. From that moment, Cain became a fugitive. He lost a glorious destiny.[4]

In the same way, many wicked people cause the destruction of so much good. They try to manipulate their circumstances for their benefit, and by doing this, they make others to suffer. Leaders oppressing the masses, sinners persecuting the righteous, and the rich maltreating their employees are all examples of individuals who try to determine the future by their manipulation of others.

The point is this: Man determines his destiny basically by discovering laws and rules of nature, life, and relationships which work in his favor. By adhering to these rules, more often than not he enjoys the natural consequences of doing the right things. However, if a man does the wrong things and keeps on manipulating his way out of the consequences thereof (thinking in his heart that he can get away with anything he does), he may only succeed for a while. Others will suffer needlessly for his acts of wickedness for a while, but ultimately, he will reap destruction.

"The wicked are proud and make evil plans to hurt the poor, who are caught in their traps and made to suffer. Those greedy people brag about the things they want to get. They curse the LORD and show that they hate him. The wicked are too proud to ask God for help. He does not fit into their plans. They succeed in everything they do. They don't understand how you can judge them. They make fun of all their enemies. They say to themselves, 'Nothing bad will ever happen to us. We will have our fun and never be punished.' They are always cursing, lying, and planning evil things to do. They hide just outside the villages, waiting to kill innocent people, always

---

[4] Genesis 4:1-13

I Determine My Own Destiny (Caution, My Dear!)

looking for any helpless person they can hurt. They are like lions hiding in the bushes to catch weak and helpless animals. They lay their traps for the poor, who are caught in their nets. Again and again they hurt people who are already weak and suffering. They say to themselves, 'God has forgotten about us. He is not watching. He will never see what we are doing.' LORD, get up and do something. Punish those who are wicked, God. Don>t forget those who are poor and helpless. The wicked turn against God because they think he will not punish them.» [5]

There is a force at work in our world beyond us which ensures that we end up reaping the rewards of every action, whether good or bad. You are not in charge; you are never in charge, and that should make you humble.

"*God has spoken once, Twice I have heard this: That power belongs to God. Also, to You, O Lord, belongs mercy; For You render to each one according to his work.*" [6]

---

5   Psalm 10:2-13 (ERV)
6   Psalm 62:11-12 (NKJV)

CHAPTER 7
HOW TO FULFILL YOUR DESTINY - A

Life is not easy, and that does not seem fair. Life wasn't meant to be difficult, either. Though life sometimes can be tougher than one can bear, it is noteworthy that for everything in life, there is always at least one easy way.

"*The way of a fool is right in his own eyes: but he who heeds counsel is wise.*"[1]

"*The labor of fools wearies them, for they do not even know how to go to the city.*"[2]

---
1   Proverbs 12:15 (NKJV)
2   Ecclesiastes 10:15 (NKJV)

The Concept of Destiny

I may not have all the answers, but we can take a critical look at the scriptures to help us in our analyses.

We will begin with the story of the Israelites. They were people who had a prophecy concerning them more than four centuries before. God promised Abraham that He would give him Canaan for a possession. He told him that his descendants would go into slavery in Egypt, but after 400 years they would be delivered and restored to the land where he had settled in for a possession.

The Israelites became slaves in Egypt, and then Moses came to deliver them. However, despite the prophecy concerning that generation and the intention of God towards them, they all perished in the wilderness except for Joshua and Caleb. It was the younger generation who did not experience slavery in Egypt that made it to the promised land.

Only the descendants of Moses, Caleb, and Joshua would have entered the Promised Land if Moses had not interceded for the people. [3]

Here we see the sovereign God, with great intention and a wonderful plan, failing to achieve His intention with the original people for whom He planned it. He got them out of Egypt but could not get Egypt out of them. He revealed Himself to them and tried to establish a relationship with them, but they just could not understand nor trust Him. They grieved Him many times and walked in unbelief.

Did God achieve His purpose or intention? In other words, did the descendants of Abraham possess the land promised them? Yes. Did it happen to the generation for whom He planned it? No. Did it happen exactly the way God planned it? No. God had to keep working things out each time they messed up His plans. This reveals the faithfulness of God to His word and His love for mankind, as well as the fact that man has the will to decide whether to follow God's purpose for him or not.

---

3   Numbers chapters 13-14

Some of the lessons from the story:

1. God has an intention for your existence, and therefore has a purpose for your life.
2. God expects your cooperation for the smooth fulfilment of His plan in such a perfect way as the original intention, and that makes your life a passing phase in the eternal picture of the universe. Your lifetime is just a period in the whole of eternity.
3. God is committed to your success because it will bring Him glory.
4. The troubles you pass through are either part of His plan or a result of your own wrong decisions.

   If it is part of His plan, it is a challenge meant to make you stronger and will catapult you faster to your place in destiny. He will have a solution waiting, and you only need to look up to Him in trust. A good example is Paul and Silas in the prison, where they prayed and worshipped God; there was an earthquake, the doors flew open, the jailer and his household believed in Christ Jesus, and they were released and acquitted from all charges the next morning.

   If it is due to your wrongdoing, the journey becomes filled with curves and not as straight as it should be. Yet God tries to find an alternative way to work all things out for your good. An example is when Abram went down to Egypt, and God had to defend him by keeping Sarai safe in Pharaoh's palace.

In summary, many times we are the cause of the troubles we pass through. Even amid all our troubles, God is with us and sees us through if we will depend on him.

"And we know that for those who love God all things work together for good, for those who are called according to his purpose."[4]

---
4   Romans 8:28 (ESV)

CHAPTER 8
HOW TO FULFILL YOUR DESTINY - B

You need guidance!

"He makes me to lie down in green pastures: he leads me beside the still waters. He restores my soul; he leads me in the paths of righteousness for his name's sake." [1]

God spoke to Abraham, "Follow Me, and I will make you great." He took off immediately and followed the Lord with enthusiasm. Abraham had grown up in a land with many gods where they literally had an idol for everything. He had no

---

[1] Psalm 23:2-3 (NKJV)

The Concept of Destiny

scriptures to read and no one who knew this God who could guide him. All he had was an unseen God who was talking to him, both audibly and most especially in his heart. This contrasted with the idols who had eyes but could not speak and limbs but could not move.

Abraham did not always listen to God. There were times when he went off on his own and had to use his own wisdom for survival. The first time was when he got to Canaan and there was a famine. With all the fanfare and joy with which he followed God, the first thing he had to face was famine, and that was strange and difficult for him to fathom. Abraham's instinct for survival took him to Egypt, where he adopted street-smart techniques so he would not be lynched. God allowed him but preserved him through it all and brought him up again to himself. Note that all the while he was in Egypt, there is no record that God spoke to Abraham; rather, God was speaking to Pharaoh. God seemed to always allow Abraham to have his way each time he went off alone but was busy cleaning up the mess because of His promise. I guess every good parent does that for their children.

Through that adventure in Egypt, he came out with Haggai, who later had a child for him in another event in which God was a spectator but had to clean up another mess! Till today, the descendants of Ishmael are still a thorn in the flesh of Isaac. They are noted all through history to be in strife with Israel on a persistent basis.

For Isaac, it was different. There was a famine, just like in the time of his father. Isaac, however, under the tutelage of his dad, had learned the importance of meditation and divine guidance. Thus, he communed with God about his intentions and God told him, "Do not go down to Egypt; dwell in this land, because what makes the difference is My presence" (*paraphrased*). Isaac made different decisions, and he prospered far more than his father did in similar circumstances. *

How To Fulfill Your Destiny - B

Lessons from the story:

1. There is a plan in God's mind concerning you: God had a plan for both Abraham and Isaac which was going to affect their generation. There is a high probability that He has the same for you. No manufacturer creates a thing without first determining the purpose and the design in his imagination.

2. God's plan is the perfect route to His purpose for us: God's plan is perfect, though it includes difficulties which He allows so we can relate with Him in faith, and He can manifest His power on our behalf.

3. Not everything in our lives is exactly God's plan: Each time we go off on our own, He allows us. Whenever we miss it and we come back to Him, he resolves the difficulties and works things out for our good.

4. He never fails us: God never changes His purpose, and the end He planned for us will materialize if we do not give up on Him. Any roughness in our journey is likely to be due to our errors, ignorance, imperfections, stubbornness, or simplicity, yet He knows how to work things around to put us back on the right path.

"And we know that for those who love God all things work together for good, for those who are called according to his purpose."[2]

*Read Genesis chapters 12-17

---

2 Romans 8:28 (ESV)

CHAPTER 9
HOW TO FULFILL YOUR DESTINY - C

You are the featured actor in the movie of your life.

Moses was born at a perilous time, but his parents saw something in the child which made them risk their lives to preserve him. The boy grew up being nourished by the resources of the person who would have killed him. It takes great courage, and it is an act of faith for anyone to do what his parents did at that time. So, we could say that Moses was a product of faith.*

As he grew up, he saw the sufferings and the reproach of his people and had the urge to do something about it. By the time he was forty years old, having accomplished as much as a general in

The Concept of Destiny

Pharaoh's army, "mighty in words and deeds,"[1] Moses could not restrain himself anymore. In a quiet way, he began a revolution which he expected his own people to rally round him to accomplish; but to the contrary, they distanced themselves from him.*

Moses got in trouble after he killed and buried an Egyptian and he ran away. With all his vision and passion, Moses became a fugitive. It was forty years later that God sought Moses out in the wilderness, while he was working as a shepherd tending his father-in-law's sheep. He who had been born a ruler was in the wilderness with the sheep. God got his attention using the burning bush which was not consumed. That day, he got a fresh commission from God, and his task was to get the Israelites out of slavery. It was time for the divine prophecy (an agenda of over 400 years) to be accomplished. Moses succeeded in getting the children of Israel out of Egypt, but he could not get them into the promised land. He handed it over to Joshua to complete the rest of the mission **

---

[1] Acts of the Apostles 7:20-36

How To Fulfill Your Destiny - C

Critical Analysis:

1. The concept of *time* (know your season)

By the time Moses was born, it was clear that God had a plan for him. He was born at the right time and sustained by the almighty God for a divine agenda. However, by the time he was forty years old, Israel had spent only 390 years in captivity, which was ten years before the set time for their deliverance.

"He has made everything beautiful in its time." [2]

We could say, therefore, that Moses started something ten years ahead of time. He began to make certain choices because he was zealous for his people. Those were his own decisions because God had not yet commissioned him at the time. His decision to go ahead without God, possibly out of zeal and because he did not yet have a personal relationship with Jehovah, cost the Israelites thirty extra years of suffering and made him a fugitive for forty years. There is a time of preparation. Our lives are made up of times and seasons.

2. The concept of *method* (there is a way to go about it)

By the time he returned, the Bible made it clear that he had "known God's way" and was the meekest man on the earth. He had become submissive to doing things and approaching every issue the way God wanted it. This had become his habit, and nothing ruffled him. Each time we submit to doing things in God's way, God is honoured and glorified. Each time we don't, we are taking a risk with His purpose and our place in it.

Each time there was a crisis, and each time the people had a complaint, Moses called on the Lord and received direction on what to do. He received advice from others only with God's approval, and things went well. Until one fateful day, he missed it. He made a mistake that was not evident of meekness. The people's complaints had wearied him. He was no longer the gentle Moses who came back from the wilderness.

---

[2] Ecclesiastes 3:11 (NKJV)

The Concept of Destiny

We can safely assume that not all that happened to him was according to the perfect plan of God. Did God fail in His purpose? No. Did it go exactly as God planned? Definitely not. What was the variable factor in all the plans? It was Moses.

Despite the forty years of training in the wilderness and the "new nature" of meekness, Moses did not enter the promised land. This was because he committed an error towards the end of the mission which cost him his place in God's plan and deprived him of a triumphant entry.

Lessons from the story:

- God has a plan for every individual who is born on the earth which may be obvious or hidden at birth.
- There is a time for the manifestation of those plans, and they may be in phases.
- Learning the ways of God becomes critical in the realization of our life purpose.
- God's calling and gifting are without repentance. You never lose your talents and skills, even if you never discover, develop, or use them.
- God seeks for us and tries to get our attention at a point in our lives. It is up to us to notice Him and give Him the required attention. For some, it takes a tragedy for God to get their attention.
- God respects our personal decisions such that ultimately, we are responsible for the execution of His purpose for us. He ensures that we are always willing and not under compulsion in the accomplishment of His purpose.

"I can of mine own self do nothing: as I hear, I judge: and my judgment is just; because I seek not mine own will, but the will of the Father which hath sent me." [3]

"Therefore doth my Father love me, because I lay down my life, that I might take it again. No man taketh it from me, but I lay it

---
3   The Gospel according to John 5:30 (KJV)

down of myself. I have power to lay it down, and I have power to take it again. This commandment have I received of my Father." [4]

You are like the featured actor in the movie of your life; ensure that you are in tune with God, the movie producer and director.

*Read Exodus chapter 1-3

**Read Deuteronomy 31:1-3 & chapter 34

---

4 The Gospel according to John 10:17-18 (KJV)

CHAPTER 10
HOW TO FULFILL YOUR DESTINY - D

You Need an Advocate

Destiny could go wrong without an advocate. Experiences in life have shown that the availability of an advocate can make a difference in ensuring that a glorious destiny does not go wrong. One way to secure an advocate is to have a mentor or to present yourself as a protégé to one who has achieved what you desire.

The children of Israel left Egypt for the promised land. The land of Canaan was their inheritance as heirs of Abraham, promised to him by God more than 400 years before this time, and at a time they were still existing in his loins. That was their destiny—to become God's own nation. A people redeemed, and a special nation on the earth. Although they left Egypt, they carried Egypt in their hearts. God got them out of Egypt, but He could not get Egypt out of their hearts. Each day, they missed Egypt and could not focus on the goal before them. They doubted God's ability to fulfil His promises and often grumbled and complained. A time came when God decided to destroy them and create a new generation of Israelites through Moses, but Moses refused. He became their advocate, and they were spared. [1]

Peter was a beloved disciple of Christ. As Jesus neared the end of His ministry, He told Peter, "Satan desired thee, to sift thee as wheat, but I have prayed for you that your faith fail not." Peter, who betrayed Jesus soon after that, was able to find his way back to God through repentance, because his faith did not fail. Jesus, as an advocate, preserved Peter's divine destiny as an apostle of Christ. [2]

Parents who are discerning can serve as effective advocates for their children by standing in the place of prayer, interceding for

---
1 Numbers 14:10-20
2 Luke 22:31-34

them. Many glorious destinies have been lost because of parents who did not understand the importance of advocacy. Jacob knew the importance of a name. His name was changed before he experienced the full manifestation of God's blessings. This experience at a critical point in his life taught him how the pronunciations of a parent, which includes the name given to a child, could influence a man's destiny. So, when Rachel called her son "Ben-Oni," meaning "the son of my sorrow," Jacob instantly changed the boy's name to "Benjamin," meaning "the son of my right hand." Thus, he secured and ensured a beautiful destiny for Benjamin. [3]

Daniel was in captivity in Babylon. Yet he knew that the time was near for them to be delivered from exile and restored back to Jerusalem. Daniel therefore decided to pray. Advocacy, or intercession, was the strength of Daniel. All through his life, he had enjoyed tremendous breakthroughs and a successful political career through the acts of intercession. So, one more time, he set his face to seek God's face concerning his homeland. From the moment he knelt to pray, God heard him and sent a reply.[4] God will hear you today if you will pray for your life, your glorious destiny, and for your loved ones.

The Role of Advocacy

Advocacy can only deliver what grace has made available. In life, as you live each day, if all you can achieve will be by your strength alone, you will be limited in many ways. God has made sure that each destiny is not limited by virtue of birthplace, family status, race, physical talents, or abilities. Every child is born equal: naked, and we all depart naked. The difference will be what we accomplish here on earth, and how we live. Grace is made available to everyone who will make use of it. It enables us to overcome our limitations.

Sodom and Gomorrah had no existing covenant with God. They were entrenched in sin and wickedness, so much so that

---

3   Genesis 35:16-18
4   Daniel 9:2-3, 20

heaven singled them out for destruction. Alas, Lot was living in Sodom. Lot found grace because he was Abraham's nephew. Abraham became an advocate for Sodom and Gomorrah, for Lot's sake. Grace was available for Lot and his family and their associates. Grace was not available to the other inhabitants of the land. Abraham's advocacy worked for Lot and his family, and for his in-laws, but the rest of the city perished. [5]

Parents, children, have served as advocates for families. Individuals have served as advocates for cities and nations. Advocacy preserves destinies. Advocacy works. But advocacy only delivers what grace has made available. Finding oneself in a perilous situation without an advocate can result in a truncated destiny. Samuel was sad about the fate of King Saul. He spent many days praying for him, but grace was not available for Saul. Grace was not available for Saul because he failed to humble himself before God, but rather preferred to please the people. [6]

"God resisteth the proud, but giveth grace unto the humble." [7]

David also sinned, but David experienced grace because he humbled himself. To ensure that a man ends well in the journey of life, divine grace is inevitable. It works every time.

So, we see that grace can be courted primarily through relationships. The primary grace given to a child is the parents. The primary grace given to a husband is the wife, and vice versa. So, grace is also given to citizens of a county, state, or nation by virtue of identification as citizens, and the same grace is not available to foreigners. You can increase the grace upon your life by creating and sustaining great relationships. You can increase in grace; you can reduce in grace; and you can maximize grace or frustrate grace. Sometimes, grace is referred to as "goodwill."

An example of someone who frustrated the grace upon his life is Samson. He had every opportunity to retrace his steps

---

5   Genesis 18:22-19:25
6   1 Samuel 15:20
7   James 4:6 (KJV)

when he did wrong. His parents advised him not to go after strange women, but he did not listen. Every sign was there for him to realize that danger was looming, but he was blinded by lust. Someone who maximized grace was the apostle Paul.

"For I am the least of all the apostles... but I laboured more abundantly than they all: yet not I, but the grace of God which was with me." [8]

Do you acknowledge the graces in your life? Are you grateful for them? Are you laboring with grace and maximizing the graces in your life, or are you frustrating them and wasting them? Like Paul—a lawyer, a Roman citizen, a respected Pharisee, a successful businessman, an excellent orator, and an erudite speaker—many of us are endowed with a lot of grace. While we are endowed with so much grace naturally, what tops it all and guarantees an enviable destiny for an individual is divine grace, received from God the Creator of all.

---

[8] 1 Corinthians 15:9-10 (KJV)

CHAPTER 11
HOW TO FULFILL YOUR DESTINY - E

Be in the right position.

You are an eternal being. The life force within you, your spirit man, lives forever. Being on earth is a passing phase. Your life on earth is a snapshot in eternity. The eternal God made man and placed us in "time" to fulfill a purpose. Afterwards, we move out of the limited time phase into eternity. Your satisfaction in life will come out of the feeling that you have fulfilled your purpose here. Ultimately, it will not be how many things you possessed, or how much you achieved, but how fulfilled you are with the important issues of life and destiny.

"Rejoice, O young man, in thy youth; and let thy heart cheer thee in the days of thy youth, and walk in the ways of thine heart, and in the sight of thine eyes: but know thou, that for all these things God will bring thee into judgment." [1]

God the Creator loves all His creation. If a man works diligently with the laws and principles of life, he has a good chance to succeed in what he does. We do not necessarily need a direct allegiance with God to succeed in life. Success as defined by man varies from individual to individual, and from culture to culture. Success does not translate to fulfillment of purpose or satisfaction with life. For us to fulfill our life's purpose, or our God-ordained destiny, God has made divine grace available to us all. This grace is available in Christ Jesus.

"And of his fulness have all we received, and grace for grace. For the law was given by Moses, but grace and truth came by Jesus Christ." [2]

---

1   Ecclesiastes 11:9 (KJV)
2   John 1:16-17 (KJV)

Take position in Christ.

Those who are in Christ have a glorious destiny by virtue of their position in Him. Christ is like a vehicle, conveying men to eternal life. "He that believeth in him shall not perish but have everlasting life." Also, the scriptures say that He ever lives to make intercession/advocacy for us, and that He can save to the uttermost all that come to God by him. [3]

In the same way that you enter an airplane going to Washington, if you want to get to Washington, the same way the life expectancy differs from country to country and affects those in that particular location; taking a position in Christ has its guarantees. Through Him and in Him we are transformed into spiritual beings, connected to our Maker, and able to make this world a better place. In Christ, we have hope not only in this world, but in the world to come.

"But as many as received him, to them gave he power to become the sons of God, even to them that believe on his name: Which were born, not of blood, nor of the will of the flesh, nor of the will of man, but of God." [4]

"Ye are a chosen generation, a royal priesthood, an holy nation, a peculiar people." [5]

So many good things are written concerning those who are in Christ. They are new creatures, free from all condemnation. They have a glorious heritage, they become joint heirs with Christ and heirs of the kingdom of God. As sons of God, filled with the Spirit of God, all things in their life work together for good. To experience all these promises, all a man needs to do is to come unto God and become "in Christ." [6]

In addition to ensuring a glorious and enviable destiny, God has also made Jesus Christ our advocate.

---

3   John 3:16, Hebrews 7:25
4   John 1:12 (KJV)
5   1 Peter 2:9 (KJV)
6   Romans 8:1, 28

"We have an advocate with the Father, Jesus Christ the righteous." [7]

Therefore, all those who are positioned in Christ are automatically insured, because they do not only have a glorious destiny, they have received grace to ensure they do not miss out on it, and they also have an advocate to intercede for them. It is a done deal.

"For whom he did foreknow, he also did predestinate to be conformed to the image of his Son, that he might be the firstborn among many brethren. Moreover, whom he did predestinate, them he also called: and whom he called, them he also justified: and whom he justified, them he also glorified." [8]

What are you waiting for? We need the grace of God to be satisfied and fulfilled in life. I do not define success by men's standards. Many successful people have ended up miserable. To be successful is to be fulfilled; that is, to have this inner satisfaction that you are fulfilling your purpose for living. Many live their lives without this sense of satisfaction.

"Behold, what manner of love the Father hath bestowed upon us, that we should be called the sons of God... Beloved, now are we the sons of God, and... we know that, when he shall appear, we shall be like him; for we shall see him as he is." [9]

---

7   1 John 2:1 (KJV)
8   Romans 8:29 (KJV)
9   1 John 3:1-2 (KJV)

CHAPTER 12
WHAT IS WRITTEN CONCERNING YOU?

How much about you do you know?

To fulfill your destiny, you need to be aware of what is written concerning you. There were books written concerning you before you were born, foretelling the kind of person you would look like, the temperament you would display, how intelligent you would be, and how you would make decisions.

The Concept of Destiny

Let us briefly examine each of those books.

1. Your genes

Written in every cell in your body is a book. This book is coded within the inner chambers of your cells, called the *nucleus*. In its coded form, this book is known as *genes*. When decoded, all the information within it could fill a whole library. The intricate way in which the genes are packed and made so tiny and microscopic still baffles scientists, but being able to decode the human genome was one of the greatest achievements of the 20th century.

Your genes say a lot about you. How tall you will become, the color of your eyes, your temperament, your talents, your ability to develop new skills, the possible types of diseases you can develop, how long you will live, and much more could be determined by studying your genes.

The big deal is this: you alone carry the blueprint in your genes. They are unique to you alone. There may be similarities, but none is exactly like yours. It is the same with identical twins, as their genes are not exact copies. You are specially wrought by creation at conception.

"For you formed my inward parts; you knitted me together in my mother's womb. I praise you, for I am fearfully and wonderfully made. Wonderful are your works; my soul knows it very well. My frame was not hidden from you, when I was being made in secret, intricately woven in the depths of the earth. Your eyes saw my unformed substance; <u>in your book were written,</u> every one of them, the days that were formed for me, when as yet there was none of them. How precious to me are your thoughts, O God! How vast is the sum of them! If I would count them, they are more than the sand. I awake, and I am still with you." [1]

2. God's books

Your Creator has a book written concerning you. As your

---
[1] Psalm 139:13-18 (ESV)

What is Written Concerning You?

manufacturer, He has a manual, detailing what He created you for and the capacity given to you achieve it. The book contains a diagnostic section which reveals the signs that show you are about to malfunction, and how to get you repaired. It talks about reset buttons. The book even talks about each day of your life, before you had even lived one of it.

"In your book were written, every one of them, the days that were formed for me, when as yet there was none of them."[2]

There are two books God has written concerning you (apart from the one in your cells!). Isn't that wonderful? The problem with the first book is that it is coded. It barely makes sense on a literal view, and many misinterpretations have come out of it. The good news is that the second book is for decoding the first book.

The first book is the Holy Bible. I assure you that a lot of things are written concerning you in the Holy Bible, and you will do yourself a lot of good regardless of your creed or race to take time to read it with an open mind.

"Then said I, Lo, I come (in the volume of the book it is written of me,) to do thy will, O God."[3]

The decoder for the Bible has been placed in your heart.

"He has made everything beautiful in its time. Also, he has put eternity into man's heart."[4]

Did you just read that? In your heart God Himself has placed another book, which helps you understand the one written (in codes) by His Holy Spirit through the hands of men. You need to clear your brain, open your mind, and engage your heart while reading the Bible, as you sincerely search for the truths written concerning you. The more you clearly see what is written concerning you from scripture, the more of what you

---

2   Psalm 139:18 (ESV)
3   Paul's Letter to the Hebrews 10:7 (KJV)
4   Ecclesiastes 3:11 (ESV)

The Concept of Destiny

were created to be you'll become. You are to relate with God primarily in your heart.

3. Third party books

These are books written concerning you by men. Part of this was written ages before you were born, by your ancestors. Your race, their location, their decisions, and much more has already been written, and you share these characteristics by virtue of your birth. Your chapter in those books started on the day you were conceived.

They decided the place of your birth, the name you would bear, and you grew up in that tutelage. The constitution of your country was written concerning its citizens, of which you are a part. Ignorance of the law is not a defense, as you are bound by the law of the land where you choose to live. All these are books written concerning you by men. This third set of books includes the plans of the wicked (if any) concerning you. For example, if your parents were killed while you were a kid, that becomes part of your story.

The question is this: Are you aware of what is written concerning you and how this affects your life? Books are important, and what is written concerning you may hold a lot of weight regarding how you will end up.

"Pilate answered, What I have written I have written."[5]

God Almighty said, "All men are like grass and the glory thereof as the flower of the field; the grass withers and the flowers fade, but My word abides forever."[6]

Are you aware of what is written concerning you? Remember, ignorance is no defense. Are you fulfilling your destiny?

We will be talking about the most important book in the next few pages.

---

5   The Gospel according to John 19:22 (KJV)
6   Isaiah 40:6-8

CHAPTER 13
THE MOST IMPORTANT VARIABLE IN THE EQUATION OF YOUR LIFE

**You are most important; you are the focus—
stop looking outward.**

Scientists discovered something important in mathematics. It was discovered that energy often dissipates into less useful energy, till it becomes zero useful energy. There was a sort of "constant" variation in the depletion. They also noticed that anything which would be sustained must have a "constant" supply of resource or replenishment.

The Concept of Destiny

For example, the only constant thing about a living thing is that "life" continuously flows through them. The moment "life" stops flowing, every living thing dies. Thus, there is a constant factor which sustains life, and that is the only consistent and reliable thing about living. The constant factor in the journey of life which sustains all there is, keeping them from extinction and doing so with so much intricate design and organization, is God—the Creator.

Every other thing in the equation of your life is a variable. Your location can change, relationships can come to an end, jobs can change, career can change, and you can even change your citizenship from one country to another. You may not be able to move God nor influence Him. There may be a limit to how much you can influence other people or make them do your bidding, but you have power over your own decisions, and that means a lot in the equation.

There are things you cannot change, no matter how many times you try. There are things which, if you tamper with them, you may succeed for a while, but at the end you become a fool. However, there is a lot you can change about yourself. The best thing you can do for yourself is to take responsibility for your decisions.

Stop blaming your location, your spouse, your citizenship, your parents, your lack of money, and your natural tendencies or weaknesses. Until you begin to work on "me," "myself," and "I," and choose to own your own part of the story, you have not taken charge of your own destiny. Note that often, God's ways are set. and all you need is to discover them and walk in them. Stop making assumptions for God. He is not subject to your imagination. Also, note that there are people with less opportunities than yourself who are doing far better. They aren't just lucky; they have a different spirit (attitude).

Note that a whole generation of Israelites left Egypt under the guidance of Moses. They had been predestined more than 400 years before to leave Egypt in grand style and cross over to

The Most Important Variable

Canaan. At the end of the journey, only two out of that generation made it across the wilderness into the promised land. These two made it because they had a different "spirit."

"*Then the LORD said, 'I have pardoned, according to your word. But truly, as I live, and as all the earth shall be filled with the glory of the LORD, none of the men who have seen my glory and my signs that I did in Egypt and in the wilderness, and yet have put me to the test these ten times and have not obeyed my voice, shall see the land that I swore to give to their fathers. And none of those who despised me shall see it. But my servant Caleb, because he has a <u>different spirit</u> and has followed me fully, I will bring into the land into which he went, and his descendants shall possess it.'"*[1]

---

[1] Numbers 14:20-24 (ESV)

CHAPTER 14
WHICH IS THE MOST IMPORTANT BOOK TO BE WRITTEN ABOUT YOU?

The complete story of your life is the real deal.

The most important book of your life is composed of the real events documented from the moment you were born till your last breath.

Previously, I wrote about books written concerning you. I emphasized the importance of knowing what is written concerning you, because your ignorance could harm you. I made it clear that much had been written concerning you even before you were born. However, please note that it is not everything written concerning you that is important. Let me tell you about the most important book which will ever be written concerning you.

The most important book is the one you write with your daily living. Not the one you write with your own hands (which may be doctored), or the one written by people about you (which will also be biased), but the complete record, taken from the day you were born till the moment you died. This record is being kept by heaven.

The Concept of Destiny

All your hidden thoughts, the secret things you did, the intention behind your actions, the sources of your motivation, and all the spiritual components (which you may not be aware of) are all being written down and kept. I shudder to think that the record is not just handwritten but may have audiovisuals as well.

This final book is not likely to be as exact as the original plan of God for you. This final book will contain records of how men and other forces influenced the events and the direction of your life. This final book will bring together all the contents of the other books in such a way as to harmonize their interplay towards the conclusion of your life. This book will be closed at the same moment you close your eyes in death. This is the most important book to be written about you.

At the end of your life, all that will matter is the final book written concerning you. The best of that book would be the one that is as close as possible to the original one God wrote about you before you were born. The most important thing is that no matter the errors, the difficulties, and the sufferings you experience in life, ensure you end well. Ensure you end well the way God intended it. That is very crucial.

Let us look at a few examples:

Abraham: Retrospectively, we are aware that when God called Abram, all He had in mind was Isaac. That was the seed of promise. Giving birth to Isaac at a specific time in history was vital, and Abraham had to be prepared for this event. He fulfilled this purpose. At the end of his life, Abraham had seven children from three women. He achieved God's purpose but also did some other things which I bet you he wished he had not done. The constant factor in his life: God. The variable: him.

Joseph: God had a great plan for Joseph. He was to become a ruler of a great nation. His destiny was great, but his brothers, Potiphar, Potiphar's wife, and a host of others had roles to play in his life. He kept making the right decisions through it all. He fulfilled his purpose. Do you remember the way he handled his brothers when they went to Egypt to buy food? That was purely Joseph in action, testing and proving whether his brothers had changed. The constant factor: God. The variable/determinant factor: Joseph. He ended well.

Samson: God raised up a great deliverer for Israel in the person of Samson. When he maintained his covenant with God, he prospered. God honored his prayers from the beginning to the end. Samson obviously did not end up the way God intended. He did not live out the conclusion of what God originally planned for him. We never got to know what was originally written concerning him, because all we could read was what he "wrote" by his own actions. He did not have an enviable end.

Saul: Saul was the first king of Israel. If Saul had done well, we may not have heard anything about David. Saul lost the throne and died an untimely death. Jonathan (and his descendants) missed out on what his destiny was meant to be by virtue of his birth as the first son of Saul and heir to the throne. The constant: God, the variable: Saul.

David: We do not know in full detail what God had planned for David. It obviously did not go exactly the way it was written concerning him by God. We only have the privilege of reading what happened. He missed it several times. Three of those times include: when he left the shores of Israel and stayed in Ziklag (he lost everything and almost lost his life), when he committed adultery with Bathsheba (he almost lost his throne, apart from Satan getting a foothold into his home and causing a lot of rebellion and killing his children), and when he decided to do a census of God's own people (which was against God's law).

The good thing about David, and a lesson for us, is that if we turn back to God and are submissive to Him, He will work all things (inclusive of all our errors and incompetence) out for our good. The fact that He uses it all to make a good ending in our lives does not necessarily imply that He allowed all those sufferings in the first place. Sometimes we suffer the consequences of

The Concept of Destiny

our actions, and those lessons make us better people, but it was we who caused the error in the first place; God just stepped in to clear the mess.

Ensure you end well the way God intended it. That is the most important thing.

"How can a young man keep his way pure? By guarding it according to your word. With my whole heart I seek you; let me not wander from your commandments! I have stored up your word in my heart, that I might not sin against you. Blessed are you, O LORD; teach me your statutes! With my lips I declare all the rules of your mouth" (Psalm 119:9-13 ESV).

Shalom!

YOU WERE BORN A KING; DO NOT DIE A PEASANT!

Take responsibility for your life.

From the scriptures, we understand that before coming forth into the world, everyone has a predestined end. This goes with the concept of a Creator who has a purpose for everything He created. He created us in his own image, and no man builds a house he has not imagined; neither do we lay the foundation for a monument without a purpose. In the same vein, God the Creator is not oblivious of any human being conceived at any time. He does have a purpose for you.

The Concept of Destiny

"My flesh was made by you, and my parts joined together in my mother's body. I will give you praise, for I am strangely and delicately formed; your works are great wonders, and of this my soul is fully conscious. My frame was not unseen by you when I was made secretly, and strangely formed in the lowest parts of the earth.

"Your eyes saw my unformed substance; in your book all my days were recorded, even those which were purposed before they had come into being. How dear are your thoughts to me, O God! how great is the number of them! If I made up their number, it would be more than the grains of sand; when I am awake, I am still with you." [1]

Your conception and birth were not mistakes!

By virtue of the process of conception and delivery, no one was made to survive in a vacuum. The essence of the family and the community is to nurture us till we can survive on our own. Thus, we are influenced by our national and communal history, influenced by the norms and values of society, and influenced largely by the decisions those on whom we are dependent in our early years make on our behalf. Sometimes they decide to abort the child (and abort God's purpose with it), but some children still survive that.

As you age, become responsible.

Sooner or later, the time comes when you begin to make your own decisions. At that time, you must begin to take responsibility for your decisions. Good parents prepare their children for that eventuality, and good children listen to their parents.

Life respects a man who can define what he wants and is ready to go for it. Until you stop pointing at your circumstances as an excuse for your failure, or at other people as being responsible for your situation, you are not being responsible. Maturity is

---
1   Psalm 139:13-17 (BBE)

when you accept responsibility for the outcome of your decisions. When you develop the ability to determine what exactly your goals in life should be and develop a strategy for pursuing them, you have done one very important thing in life.

It is never too early nor too late to make a change that will steer you in the right direction. Abraham was called at seventy-five years old. Samuel began to hear God speak as a child. Joseph had his dreams at a tender age. David was anointed king as a teenager. When a smoker stops smoking, the impact of not smoking is felt in his body within twelve hours. When an individual turns to God and commits his life to Him, he is transformed instantly and set up for glory and honor. All who are in Christ are destined for glory.

God is willing to reveal to you his purpose for your life.

God is committed to your success because your success will bring glory to Him. God has done all that is necessary to give you access. Jesus Christ has paved the way for you. Now you can approach God directly, without any barrier between you and Him. He is willing to partner with you in the journey of life.

"'I say this because I know the plans that I have for you.' This message is from the LORD. 'I have good plans for you. I don't plan to hurt you. I plan to give you hope and a good future. Then you will call my name. You will come to me and pray to me, and I will listen to you. You will search for me, and when you search for me with all your heart, you will find me. I will let you find me.'" [2]

Engage your heart in the search for the living God. If you draw near to Him, God will also draw near to you. The buck does not start with you; it starts and stops with your Creator, but the ball is in your court. Ensure you play it according to the rules.

God is a constant factor.

God is a constant factor in His purpose for you. He is dependable. Those who put their trust in God will not be put to

---

2   Jeremiah 29:11-14a (ERV)

The Concept of Destiny

shame. His purposes do not change, but He may adjust His original plans as needed, and this depends on your own attitude and decisions. Other men represent a variable in your life over which you have little or no influence. The only variable in your life over which you have influence is yourself. I am positive that you will take charge and be responsible for yourself (preferably under God) and for the sake of all whose lives depend on your success.

CONTACT THE AUTHOR:

John Owoade Agboola

owoade14@gmail.com

14, Radde Place #3
Brooklyn NY 11233

www.life-indeed.fun

"Dr. John Agboola does a great job of equipping us to understand what the biblical concept of destiny is. Understanding the concept can lead us into a journey that will transform our lives and the people around us at work, in our families, and in our nations.

As you read the book, be prepared to be challenged about why you are here. How did you get here? Where you are going, and how do you find and fulfill your destiny?

The book contains important teachings that need to be embraced, internalized, and lived out practically by every child of God. It makes it clear that we are born to be kings, to reign on earth so we can bring God's glory to bear in this world."

- Dr Ayobami Adeniji, Bundaberg, Australia

"What gets me most excited about this book is the way genetics, choices, environmental factors, and scriptures are beautifully interwoven into an elegant transport medium. For example, he shows you how to decode your genes and heart using the Bible. Only a few writers are able to carry their audience on the journey of destiny discovery like Dr. John Agboola has. A highly recommended read."

- Tobi Ozoya, MD, MPH, Florida, USA

"This book is a timely piece with clear biblical examples. A must-read for the understanding and discovery of purpose."

- Abiodun Omonori, Psychiatrist, Nottingham, UK

Printed in the USA
CPSIA information can be obtained
at www.ICGtesting.com
CBHW071548200824
13468CB00061B/1255